P9-DBT-420

A World of Field Trips

Going to a Library

Rebecca Rissman

Heinemann Library
Chicago, Illinois

www.capstonepub.com
Visit our website to find out more information about Heinemann-Raintree books.

To order:
☎ Phone 800-747-4992
💻 Visit www.capstonepub.com to browse our catalog and order online.

Edited by Rebecca Rissman, Dan Nunn, and Catherine Veitch
Designed by Richard Parker
Picture research by Tracy Cummins
Originated by Capstone Global Library Ltd
Printed in the United States of America in North Mankato, Minnestoa. 082012   006887RP

15 14 13 12
10 9 8 7 6 5 4 3 2 1

Library of Congress Cataloging-in-Publication Data
Rissman, Rebecca.
 Going to a library / Rebecca Rissman.
    p. cm.—(A world of field trips)
 Includes index.
  ISBN 978-1-4329-6071-1 (hb)—ISBN 978-1-4329-6080-3 (pb)
 1. Libraries—Juvenile literature. 2. School field trips—Juvenile literature. I. Title.
 Z665.5.R57 2012
 027—dc22   2011015155

Acknowledgments
We would like to thank the following for permission to reproduce photographs: Alamy p. 16 (© Keith Morris); Corbis pp. 9 (© Shalom Ormsby/Blend Images), 10 (© Hill Street Studios/Blend Images), 11 (© Andersen Ross/Blend Images), 17 (© moodboard), 18 (© ROBERT PRATTA/Reuters), 19 (© JOCHEN LUEBKE/epa), 23b (© Andersen Ross/Blend Images); Getty Images pp. 13 (Seth Joel), 20 (Thomas Barwick), 22 (Yellow Dog Productions); istockphoto pp. 6 (© kali9), 8 (© YinYang), 12 (© 7245500); Photolibrary pp. 14 (Orteo Luis), 15 (JORGEN SCHYTTE); Shutterstock pp. 4 (© Nathan Holland), 5 (© Balic Dalibor), 7 (© Flashon Studio), 21, 23a (© Blend Images).

Front cover photograph of a teacher reading to a class reproduced with permission of Corbis (© Jim Craigmyle). Back cover photograph of librarian with children reproduced with permission of istockphoto (© Jani Bryson).

Every effort has been made to contact copyright holders of any material reproduced in this book. Any omissions will be rectified in subsequent printings if notice is given to the publisher.

Contents

Field Trips

People take field trips to visit new places.

People take field trips to learn
new things.

Field Trip to a Library

Some people take field trips
to libraries.

Libraries are places where people
go to read and learn.

computer

books

Libraries have many books. Some libraries have computers and music.

Most libraries let you borrow books.
When you are finished, you bring
them back.

Everything in a library has its special place.

Librarians help people find things in a library.

Different Libraries

This is a school library.

Pupils can come here to learn more about their school work.

This is a public library.

People can come here to read
and learn.

This is a music library.

People can come here to listen
to music.

This is a special library.

People can come here to see very old books.

How Should You Act at a Library?

In most libraries you should be quiet.

You should be careful when you take
books off the shelves.

What Do You Think?

What kind of library is this?

Look on page 24 for the answer.

Picture Glossary

 **librarian** person who works in a library. Librarians help people find what they are looking for.

 **library** place where books and recordings are kept. Most libraries allow people to borrow books.

Index

Notes to Parents and Teachers

Before reading
Explain to children that a field trip is a short visit to a new place, and that it often takes place during a school day. Ask children if they have ever taken a field trip. Tell them that libraries are places where books, computers, and other resources are kept. People can borrow resources from libraries.

After reading
- Ask children to list the types of resources they could find in a library. Guide children in a discussion about how being respectful with library resources is important since many people use them.
- Turn to pages 20–21 and talk to children about how they should behave at a library. Then take children to the school library or a community library.

Answer to page 22
It is a school library.